THE KIDS' MONEY BOOK

Earning ● Saving ● Spending ● Investing ● Donating

Jamie Kyle McGillian

Sterling Publishing Co., Inc.
New York

To Geno, for all you've taught me about love and money.
You're my best.

Library of Congress Cataloging-in-Publication Data

McGillian, Jamie Kyle.
  The kids' money book : earning, saving, spending, investing, donating
/ Jamie Kyle McGillian ; illustrated by Ian Phillips.
     p. cm.
  Includes index.
Summary: Introduces how to manage money, from earning an allowance
to budgeting to saving for college.
  ISBN 0-8069-8223-3
  1. Children—Finance, Personal—Juvenile literature. 2. Finance,
Personal—Juvenile literature. [1. Finance, Personal. 2. Money.]
I. Phillips, Ian, ill. II. Title.
HG179 .M238 2003
332.024'054—dc21

                                    2002015506

                    1 3 5 7 9 10 8 6 4 2
          Published by Sterling Publishing Co., Inc.
          387 Park Avenue South, New York, N.Y. 10016
               ©2003 by Jamie Kyle McGillian
             Distributed in Canada by Sterling Publishing
       ℅ Canadian Manda Group, One Atlantic Avenue, Suite 105
                Toronto, Ontario, Canada M6K 3E7
      Distributed in Great Britain and Europe by Chris Lloyd at Orca Book
       Services, Stanley House, Fleets Lane, Poole BH15 3AJ, England
       Distributed in Australia by Capricorn Link (Australia) Pty. Ltd.
              P.O. Box 704, Windsor, NSW 2756 Australia

                    Manufactured in China
                     All rights reserved
                 Sterling ISBN 0-8069-8223-3

CONTENTS

INTRODUCTION

Some parents say the only thing their kids know about money is how to spend it. Is that true about you? If it is, unless your guardian angel has deep pockets, you are in for trouble—because *money makes the world go 'round!*

You want to buy a snack after class, take a city bus downtown, get a bike or fix up an old car to get around, go to a concert, change to a school with an art program you like? You need, guess what—dough, bread, bucks, the long green. In other words, money!

And that's just on this side of 16. The older you get, the more important money becomes: to rent an apartment, buy a house, take a vacation, travel to a job (or two); to get an education, go out for dinner and dancing, maybe get married, take care of your family—even elderly parents (someday they could be your responsibility).

All the while, the money you earn, save, spend, borrow, pay back, invest, and donate goes from hand to hand, person to person, to the government and back again. It is what keeps our country's economy going, and helps keep the world's economy strong.

Think you'll be able to do your part? Yes, but you need to start now learning about money, and not only the spending part. Deep down, you know that— that's why you picked up this book. So now let's get to it. Your future is waiting —and it's going to be great!

Chapter One
MOMENTS IN MONEY

You don't need money for everything. Some things are free: air, water, sunsets, moonlight, lightning bugs, rainbows, snowflakes, beaches. But without money, how would we get our homes, cars, clothing, or chocolate chip cookies? Not to mention books, computers, music CDs, DVDs, and marshmallows? But thousands of years ago, there was no money. So how did people get what they needed, much less wanted? How did they survive?

A HISTORY OF MONEY

Long ago, when people needed things that others had, they bartered; that's another word for trading. If you've ever traded baseball cards with a friend, or exchanged comic books, or swapped snacks with a classmate, you have bartered. You got what you wanted or needed in exchange for something else. So, let's travel back in time thousands of years, when life was very different from what we are used to today. People lived in caves or shelters that they built themselves. They ate whatever they could catch or find. Clothing was made from animal skins. Life was a lot simpler in a lot of ways. People tended to travel in small groups as they searched for food. Sometimes, two groups would cross paths and make a trade. Maybe fresh fish for animal skins. Bartering made it possible for each group to get some of what the other group had.

SWAP AND GO

Think of how life would be now if every time you needed or wanted something, you had to swap for it: "I'll give you this sweater for those shoes." "I'll give you two pillows for a blanket." Every time you got something, you had to give up something. Your exchanges would depend on your needs and how much you had, that the other person wanted, to give in exchange.

If you think about it, bartering must have had its problems. Just imagine. What if, for example, you wanted food, but you had nothing that the trader wanted? Or, what if you needed water or medicine very badly and the only things you had that the trader would take were cattle and animal skins (that you also needed)? If the person you were trading with knew how desperate you were for the water or the medicine, he might not make a trade unless you paid a lot (like all of your cattle or animal skins!). It might not be easy to find a third party to come and help you determine if the trade was fair. Imagine the arguments that some people had over their trades back then...and maybe still do today somewhere in the world.

MAKE A DEAL

Spent all your allowance? Short on money? Set up a barter system with your friends. What skills or stuff do you have that you can offer for trade for something you want? If your friend teaches you how to do origami, what can you teach him in exchange? If you loan your friend your camera, what can she give you in exchange? Maybe you can find someone to help you with your math homework in return for a snack or a ride on your bike. Who needs money when you can barter?

And just imagine, too, the life you'd have to lead—traveling on foot, with all your wares, eager to make a trade, but tired of hauling around all that stuff with you. You'd probably be thinking, "There's gotta be a better way."

THE ORIGIN OF MONEY

The idea of a medium of exchange, which was a common measure of value, came onto the scene. Depending on where you lived, the agreed-upon medium of exchange might be salt, animal skins, feathers, beads, or corn. Or it could be amber, eggs, ivory, cattle, seashells, tea, fish hooks, fur, and even tobacco. Cattle were one of the first and oldest forms of money. With a medium of exchange, there was something to count. It gave us a value system that we could all agree on.

But, of course, there were problems with some of these early forms of money. They often rotted, or blew away, or had to be stored and protected someplace, requiring a lot of space. That's when people began to realize that they needed some sort of "thing" that had an agreed-upon value to everyone. Something small, that would be easy to carry, and that would last....

Coins

Aha! Precious metals, like gold and silver, came to be used as money. Lydia, an ancient kingdom in what is now known as Turkey, was the first country to use gold to make "money." To honor King Croesus of Lydia, the gold coins were stamped with a lion's head. As coins became popular in other countries, pictures of their leaders were stamped on the faces of the coins.

Why were metal coins such a success?
- Coins could be different—one coin had one value, another had another value.
- Coins went wherever you went and were easy to carry.
- Coins didn't wear out, or rot, or run away.

- Coins could be limited in number, but enough could be made so that they wouldn't run out.
- Coins could be melted down to make new money.

The first metal money was used about 4,500 years ago. Use of the metal money soon began to spread through Europe and the Middle East. Then, about 1,800 years ago, the Chinese invented paper money. The paper represented an amount of money, and could be redeemed for something valuable, like gold. The paper money was much lighter to carry than the heavy coins. The paper money was also much cheaper to make than the coins.

Ancient temples were the first banks. They were considered the safest place to store money because it was believed that nobody would steal from a place of worship. Temples exchanged money from other cities, and some temples even made loans, which marks the beginning of commerce.

As travel between cities began to expand, and people began to trade more freely with other cultures, some traders began to pay people to exchange coins from other cities, and they took a fee from the money they exchanged. These people were called money changers and they were the first known bankers.

Money has evolved over time for our convenience. Some people don't even use actual cash these days. They use credit cards instead of carrying cash. And many people use their ATM debit cards to pay for things by drawing money directly out of their bank accounts. Can you imagine paper money and coins becoming a thing of the past?

MONEY TIMELINE

Money didn't happen overnight. The idea and then the making and different uses of money took thousands of years. Here's a quick timeline to bring you up to date.

Note: Dates up to the year 1331 are circa, meaning "approximate."

9000–6000 B.C.
Cattle and crops are used as money. Cattle are the oldest known form of money.

1200 B.C.
Mollusks called cowries are used as currency in China.

687 B.C.
First coins are invented in Lydia, Asia Minor.

600–570 B.C.
Coin usage spreads from Lydia to Greece. Before this, the Athenians used iron nails as money.

118 B.C.
Leather money is introduced into China. It consists of pieces of white deerskin with colorful borders.

At a Glance

| 9000–6000 B.C. | 1200 B.C. | 600–570 B.C. | 1160–1200 | 1236 |

10

1160–1200

Wooden sticks, or tallies, are used as credit receipts in England. Notches representing a certain amount of money are cut into the stick. The stick is then split down the middle, one part serving as a receipt for the creditor, the other a reminder for the debtor, who owes the amount.

1232–1253

Gold coins are issued by several Italian states.

1236

The Mongol empire issues paper money.

1319–1331

Parts of India and Japan issue paper money.

1440

The modern press is invented by the printer Gutenberg.

1452–1519

Money is made, using the designs of artist Leonardo de Vinci and a water-driven mill.

1500 POTLACH

Potlach (the origination of "pot luck") festivities were one of the customs of the native peoples of the American Northwest. The ceremonial occasion consisted of dancing, feasting, and an elaborate gift exchange where the tribes and participants tried to outdo each other. At some point, laws were passed and the extravagant traditional gift-giving (expensive fabrics, jewelry, and other priceless items) was stopped.

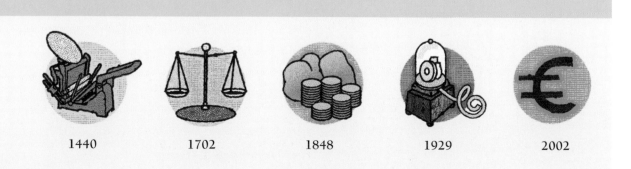

1440   1702   1848   1929   2002

1535 WAMPUM

The best-known form of money among Native Americans was wampum, made from clam shells. Strings of the beads were used for money as well as ornamentation by many North American Indians. The Indian word wampum means "white," the color of the beads. By 1637, the Massachusetts Bay Colony had declared wampum to be legal tender (okay to be used as money).

1566
In England, the Royal Exchange is built, demonstrating the importance of banking.

1599
Pepper becomes a valued commodity, sometimes worth more than its weight in gold. The Dutch try to corner the pepper market.

1702
Sir Isaac Newton, director of the London mint, assays the value of 56 different foreign silver and gold coins (finding the percentage of impurities in precious metal) relative to the British standard.

1715
Due to British coinage shortages, in North Carolina and other parts of North America wampum, tobacco, and other natural resources are used as money substitutes.

1793
The U.S. Mint begins making money for circulating, producing 11,178 copper pennies.

1848
The California Gold Rush results in a massive increase in the production of gold coins.

1909
Abraham Lincoln is put on the new American penny, marking the 100th anniversary of his birth.

DID YOU KNOW

Many of today's coins have milled, or ridged, edges. Putting ridges around coins started long ago, when coins were made of gold and silver. Certain people, at that time, would secretly shave pieces off the edges of the coins—and sell the shavings! When this "shrinking" of the coins was noticed, ridges became part of the manufacture of coins made with precious metals and stopped the thieves.

1929

A massive stock market crash, on Black Monday, causes billions of dollars to disappear from the American economy and 4,000 banks to fold.

1992

A single European market is set up to lift barriers to capital, labor, goods, and services.

2002

The euro replaces the national coinages of twelve European countries.

A MONEY STORY TO YAP ABOUT

Years ago, the natives of Yap in the South Pacific solved the problem of stolen money—no one could snatch coins that weighed close to a thousand pounds!

No, the Yap islanders didn't use gold or silver. The money was made from nothing but rock. Yap money rocks often weighed 500 pounds or more and were pounded and scraped into shape. A hole was then drilled by hand through the center of each limestone money rock so it could be moved or carried—by placing a long heavy pole through the center. The stones were moved to Yap Island from the island of Palau, some 250 miles away. The islanders would travel to Palau in open canoes and ferry the stones back on wooden rafts.

Acquiring the large stones was hard and dangerous work, but Yap tradition and culture placed great importance on the hard work of actually "making money." Stone money continues to be used by the small population of Yap islanders. For these people, stone money remains the pride of the people and a celebration of the hardships endured by their ancestors.

Chapter Two

MONEY MATTERS

How much does money matter in your life? Is it all you think about? What about when you grow up? Do you dream of going to fine restaurants and traveling around the world? Or are you afraid you will owe money, have to scrimp to put food on the table, and never be able to buy something new?

Test your money sense—your making and spending skills—with this quiz. There are no right or wrong answers, only wise and not-so-wise choices about money. Be honest with yourself. When you're done, add up your score. Learn from your responses—it's never too early or too late to sharpen your money skills.

THE MONEY SENSE QUIZ

1 You just heard a new song on the radio. You like it so much, you...
   a. run out and buy the CD.
   b. buy every CD the band ever recorded.
   c. bug a friend to buy it so you can borrow hers.
   d. wait for the song and CD to get more radio time, to make sure you still like it before buying it.
2 You just found a $10 bill in a shoe in your closet. You'd forgotten about it! You...
   a. use it to buy school supplies.
   b. stash it in your piggy bank.

   c. treat all your friends to ice cream.

   d. put it in your college fund.

3 You find a new style of jeans you really like, but they cost more than twice the price of your regular jeans. You...

   a. refuse to buy them. You don't need new jeans at that price.

   b. wait a few weeks for a sale.

   c. look for the jeans in other stores or on the Web, to find them at a cheaper price.

   d. buy them on the spot. Good jeans are hard to find.

4 It's your birthday and you got several cash gifts. You...

   a. immediately bank half and put the other half toward buying a new pair of in-line skates.

   b. put it all in a college fund.

   c. start feeding your face by buying a huge bag of candy.

   d. bank half of it and set the rest aside to start buying holiday gifts for friends and family even though it's only March.

5 Your friend's birthday is coming up; you...

   a. chip in with other friends to give your friend a pizza party.

   b. make a scrap book or home video for your friend.

   c. spend your whole allowance on an expensive gift.

   d. take part of your allowance and buy your friend a creative and unique gift.

6 You've been saving up to buy something special—a motorized scooter, a cello, or a surfboard. When you're ready, you...

   a. buy the most expensive one you can find. You deserve it.

b. buy the cheapest one and give yourself a pat on the back for saving money.

c. buy one that's well made, safety-tested, and has all the features you want at a competitive price.

d. talk with your friends to see if anyone is selling one secondhand. It may not be new, but it works and is in pretty good condition.

7 You find a charity you like. You want to contribute, so you...

a. ask your parents for money to give to the charity.

b. volunteer your time regularly at the charity or for special events.

c. put the name of the charity in your future-donations file.

d. take part in a fundraiser, like a "walk," and make a donation from your allowance.

8 A friend of a friend tells you about the latest mystery novel; you...

a. rush to the bookstore and buy it in hardcover.

b. go to the library to take it out, or "request" it.

c. order the book, plus four more books by the author.

d. can wait until your friends finish the book. You're number four on the list.

Scoring

Add up your score. Here are the point values for each response.

1.	a = 2, b = 1, c = 4, d = 3	**5.**	a = 3, b = 4, c = 1, d = 2
2.	a = 2, b = 3, c = 1, d = 4	**6.**	a = 2, b = 1, c = 4, d = 3
3.	a = 4, b = 3, c = 2, d = 1	**7.**	a = 2, b = 4, c = 3, d = 1
4.	a = 2, b = 4, c = 1, d = 3	**8.**	a = 2, b = 4, c = 1, d = 3

What your answers mean:

1 Bugging a friend is one way to save money—and maybe lose a friend. But if you're a real music lover, you may want to buy a CD of your own to keep. There

is something to be said for giving the music a little air time before you buy, especially if you're the type who likes something when it's new but gets bored with it after a while. Your answer depends on how important music is to you.

❷ What does "found" money mean to you? Do you want to run right out and spend every last dime? Or is it a great chance to add to your college fund? Saving it, investing in your future, is the most responsible money move you could make. Spending it on something you really need works too. Treating friends to ice cream is not the smartest money move, but it's nice to do sometimes. Don't get into the habit of doing it all the time, or just to try to win friends.

❸ Hooray for you if you can walk away from those jeans. If fashion is really important to you, wait and watch for a sale, comparison shop, or go on the Internet to see if you can find them cheaper. If you hardly ever find jeans that fit you so well they make you feel "special," and you do decide to pay full price, be prepared to give up something else to make up for the extra money you've spent. You should to be able to say, "They're worth it!" and mean it.

❹ Put all your birthday loot in your college fund and you are an excellent saver. If you bank half and put the other half aside for holiday presents, you're thinking long-term and that's great. You'll be buying the gifts sooner or later anyway. Again, if you can save half and spend just half on something you've been wanting, like in-line skates or a scooter, good for you. Spending all the cash on candy and other goodies will probably net you a bellyache, and maybe even a weight problem.

❺ Create a gift, such as a birthday scrap book or video that captures highlights from the special day. Your friend will think it's special and he or she will know how much you care. The party is also a nice idea, but it means you and some friends are going to have to cough up some cash. Taking a part of your allowance to buy something you know your friend would like is fine, but spending it all means leaving yourself without any cash. What if something else comes up? You'll be beyond broke.

⑥ Did you decide to buy a well-made product that's safe and competitively priced? Great! You care about what you buy and know the value of money. The worst response is to buy the cheapest simply because it is the cheapest. You could end up with a bad product, or be scrimping on safety features and that's not smart. On the other hand, automatically buying the most expensive item available just because you can is also not smart. Cost does not always mean a better product. By talking to friends about buying something secondhand, you show you're a smart spender, trying to get the most from your money. You may also end up helping out a friend ready to "trade up."

⑦ It's okay to ask your parents for money to donate, but putting in something "from your own pocket" shows you're learning the value of money—and of giving. Volunteering your time at a charity is often even more valuable than money. So many charity organizations can really use extra help. Taking part in a fund-raising event while also donating a small amount will also make you feel good about yourself.

8 If you are the kind of reader that "inhales" books, head for the library to take it out or put in a request for it. Ask your friends to pass the book on to you when they're finished, and add it to your reading list. It will probably come out in paperback in a year or so anyway. If you can't wait, buy the hardcover book. For those who treasure books, building your own library is a good investment. But quickly ordering the book, plus four more by that author isn't smart! What happens if you don't like the book, or the way the author writes? You'll be stuck with four books you may never read!

Your Score Card

Add up the points in each answer. What's your total?

8–12 ● Never Say Hopeless!

It's not too late for you! Start now by saying out loud: "I will be smarter about money decisions. I'll get money advice from some grown-up, read up on money in books and magazines, watch consumer-oriented and financial TV shows, and start keeping track of my money." Project for the day: Get a piggy bank, and start saving.

13–17 ● Lots of Potential!

The good news is that there's always room for improvement and you can learn so much from your money mistakes. Start now by setting money goals. Save a week's allowance every month. Earn extra dollars in creative ways. How about setting up a neighborhood car wash, or a fancy lemonade stand? Take the bull by the horns and set up a college fund today.

18–24 ● Dollars and Sense Surround You!

You're doing great. Get out into the community and ask people for their best money advice. Compile it into a book. Team up with a friend and set up your own business. Try odd jobs, pet-sitting, or catering. Collect a jar of lucky pennies. Use it to cover business expenses. Nurture your money skills.

25–32 ● Money Mogul

Impressive! You're headed for success. Read money publications for more in-depth information. Record your best saving and spending ideas in a money journal. Exchange sound money ideas with friends and family. Why not do something with your money skills like raise money for your local children's hospital? How about producing a children's talent show? How much money will it take to make it happen? Make sure to treat yourself every now and then. When it comes to money, you are super savvy.

WHERE DOES IT ALL GO?

A few bucks on some video games, a couple of dollars on snacks or hair gel. Some cash for the movies, and a bite after the show. Before you know it, your pockets are empty, and there's still so much you want to buy.

Get wise about money, starting right now! If you wait until you're grown up to start thinking about how to save and make money work for you, it could end up costing you a lot of dough. Start thinking about it now, while you're still a kid, and maybe you'll head off money mistakes many people make.

Which is more costly?

Making money mistakes when you're a kid (running out of allowance, and going without a snack or the latest DVD) or making serious money mistakes when you're a grown-up (losing your car because you can't make the payments, and the bank taking your house)? Grown-ups who don't learn money sense while they are young often learn the hard way. Even if they do avoid big money mistakes, always worrying about paying bills and not having enough money "to take care of my family" is no fun. The trick to changing that kind of future is to learn about handling money while you're young.

Learn now to make smart money decisions and you'll have a better chance to lead the kind of life that you want to—you won't have money problems to bring you down.

WHAT'S IN YOUR FUTURE?

Imagine you're a grown-up. What kind of role will money play in your life? If travel is important to you, start saving now to afford those planes, trains, and cruise ships that will get you there. If you are crazy about fancy cars, think about how you are going to pay for those sharp wheels. If you like horses, what if you owned a horse ranch and one of your horses won the Kentucky Derby! Maybe you love baseball, and you'll be that someone who paid a million dollars for that one-of-a-kind team-signed ball that won the World Series. Or maybe you just want a nice big house with a huge swimming pool, and room for friends to stay and have fun when they come for the weekend.

Here are 8 ideas to help you jump-start your money smarts:

❶ Make a plan. You've looked into your future—or the future you'd like to have. How will you get there? The time to start planning is now. Keep a log, a notebook of money goals to reach by the time you turn 12, or 15, 18, or 21. Your goals will probably change as you grow. You also need to make another list—of what you can do now to help you reach your goals. Be as specific as possible.

❷ Find a money mentor, someone you trust who can give you advice about handling money. Ask this family member, or family friend who wants the

best for you, to help you put together a money plan and set realistic goals. For instance, let this person help you determine how long it will take to save for what you want. If you want a bike and it costs $200, how much can you sock away each week? Set aside a few minutes each week with your money mentor to review your money goals and talk about money.

❸ Use allowance as a dress rehearsal for the real thing. The more practice you have making money decisions, the smarter your money choices will be. Each week, imagine that you have a certain amount of money. Make up a budget. Allot some of your pretend cash for clothes, snacks, fun with friends, savings, donations, and special occasions—like holiday gifts. If you don't get an allowance, pretend that you do. If your imagination needs a little help, buy or use pretend money from an old game you don't play anymore.

5 Money Goals

1. Build up my college fund

2. Take my parents on a cruise

3. Have stylish clothes

4. Be able to donate money to what's important to me

   (wildlife conservation)

5. Own a collection of modern art

What I Need to Do

1. Save; study hard and apply for grants, loans, and scholarships

2. Set up a vacation fund now

3. Learn to be a smart shopper

4. Collect spare change in a fund, volunteer for fund-raising

   activities

5. Go to art museums, learn about modern artists, take a

   painting class

④ Know your money style. Are you a spender or a saver? For some people, saving is almost second nature. For others, spending comes way too easy. And people who know what it's like not to have much money may develop strange money habits. They may hoard all their money for fear of losing it. If you are a saver by nature, it doesn't mean you're a better person than someone who loves to spend. It does mean that you are off to a good start toward managing your money. If, by nature, you seem to be more of a spender, arm yourself with ideas and information to help you save your money. (This book should help the cause.)

⑤ Learn from your mistakes. Got ripped off? Waited too long for the price to drop on those jeans and now they're not in the store? Or maybe you got a real bargain? You will no doubt make dozens, or hundreds, make that thousands, of smart and not-so-smart choices. Many of these choices will stick with you for life and will become your own personal money stories. Share them with your friends. Learn from them by talking about what you could have done to change each outcome so that it was a smart money move.

⑥ Keep a money journal. Start it now and record your ideas and feelings about money and the things you buy or want to buy. Start with responses to: What was the last thing you bought with your own money? How did it make you feel? If you could buy anything right now, what would it be? What would you like to buy for someone else? How does spending money make you feel?

⑦ Create a money club with friends. Have each member contribute a few bucks each month. What can you buy? What can you save for? How can you invest that money to make more money? How about starting a business with your friends (see pages 32–35 for some ideas)?

⑧ Pay attention to the economy. Get in the habit of reading the finance pages in your local newspaper. Learn about companies that may be worthy of investing in. Think about how the economy affects your life. Think like a smart money manager.

KNOW THE DIFFERENCE BETWEEN NEEDS AND WANTS

How do you know the best way to spend a few bucks? Is it better to use the money to buy a couple of good books for your personal library, or should you buy some computer games? Either purchase might make you smart. But which purchase is more practical and which one will provide more enjoyment?

Everyone has his or her unique and individualized way of deciding what to buy or not buy. We are all different, but we all have to separate the things we need from the things we want.

Learning the difference between what we need and what we want is a huge step toward learning to use money wisely. You learn that you don't need to buy the huge rabbit's foot, the neon shoelaces, the cool sweatshirt, or the plastic lobster that sings when you press its belly. You learn to save money! What's the difference between your needs and your wants? Your needs are the things you must have—food, clothing, and shelter. Your wants are the things that you wish you had—concert tickets, your own private telephone line, or the very latest computer.

_____ a new outfit
_____ a pencil case
_____ expensive sneakers
_____ a gallon of glorious ice cream
_____ dance lessons
_____ bedroom furniture
_____ ice skates
_____ your favorite food at home
_____ a puppy
_____ a visit to your favorite
      clothing store
      fancy chocolates
_____ a credit card
_____ a cell phone
_____ a beeper
_____ a computer

Go through the list below and mark each item with an N for need or a W for want.

_____ three square meals a day
_____ an awesome DVD collection
_____ medicine
_____ a shopping spree at the mall
_____ a visit to the mall's food court
_____ eyeglasses or contact lenses

It's all right to have a lot of wants, but the idea is to keep them in check. Think of your wants as ice-cream sundaes. What would happen if every time you wanted a sundae, you had one? You'd probably put on pounds you don't need, and get really sick of sundaes! But, if you limit the number of times you treat yourself, when you do have a sundae: Mmmm! Is that good!

Margo

I need hugs, veggies, and fresh air.

I want a gold bracelet, hiking gear, and a sailboat.

Ryan

I need friends and family, lots of exercise, and plenty of H_2O.

I want a cell phone, skis, a cool computer, and six pairs of boots.

Julia

I need to do well in school, save money for college, and get enough sleep.

I want a tropical vacation, a new 10-speed bike, guitar lessons, and a closet filled with funky clothes.

Just as no two people are the same, no two people have exactly the same needs and wants. And these needs and wants often change. What are some of your needs and wants? Start a running list. Some of the things on your want list could vary greatly in price and value—a raspberry ice-cream cone and a shiny red convertible.

Keep a monthly record. Notice how your needs and wants change. Something high on your list now may drop to the bottom by next year. As you mature, and as your environment changes, so do your needs and wants.

Keep your wants in check by making a pact with yourself not to buy anything on your want list for an entire month. For each day you pass it up, give yourself a gold star. After the month is up, review your list. What can you cross off the list?

Add up the cost of all the items on your want list. How much money do you save if you don't give in?

ADJUST YOUR ATTITUDE—MONEY CAN'T BUY YOU LOVE

Money can buy you all sorts of things, but it can't give you a shining personality. It can't make you strong. (In fact, it can reveal your weaknesses!) It can't give you a great laugh. And it definitely can't make you a better person (unless you discover how great it feels to be generous and you use your money to make the world a better place).

So, is it a good thing or a bad thing? That depends. Take a look at the two sides of money.

When money is cool:
- When you earn it from doing hard work.
- When you spend it on someone other than yourself.
- When it brings you together with old or new friends.
- When you buy something that brings you true joy.
- When you win it.
- When you use it to help someone.
- When you find some in the pocket of your old jean jacket.
- When you're way under budget.

When money is uncool:
- When you lose it.
- When you've spent it all, even your bus fare.

- When someone owes you some.
- When you owe someone else some.
- When you fight over it with friends or a sibling.
- When someone brags about how much he or she has.
- When you start believing you can't be happy without it.
- When you're way over your budget.
- When you spend all your time trying to get more.

MONEY IS PERSONAL

People have different views about money. For some, the meaning of financial success is a big house, fancy cars, diamond rings, and everything you could ever want. For others, it's a small, comfortable hideaway on a secluded island. It's all a matter of personal choice.

When John D. Rockefeller was the richest man in the world, he was asked, "How much money is enough?" His reply was, "Just a little more."

How do you feel about those crisp bills and shiny coins? How important is having money to you? Do you think it's the key to happiness? Does it really measure success? Can you be happy without it? When you think of money, what words or images come to mind?

"I see hundreds of pieces of candy, CDs, magazines, dolls, and lots of shiny quarters."—Alex, 8

Having money is good, but did you know that money causes more problems in families and between people than anything else? The strange thing is that a lot of people don't sit down and really talk about money until it's already a big problem.

"I see tons of dollar signs swirling into one another."—Daniel, 9

Mia, a ten-year-old, recalls how money changed her life when her parents' family business became very successful.

"At first, it was like the greatest feeling in the world. We got new everything. We moved into a giant house with a bathroom for each bedroom. We got new cars, tons of toys, and all the new clothes we could possibly wear. But then everything started to change. My family got wrapped up in the idea of being rich. Too much money makes you forget what's important—friends, health, good books, long hikes, and chocolate chip ice cream."

If you and your family suddenly became very rich, how do you think your life would change? What would stay the same?

In today's hectic, fast-paced times, some people are consumed by money: "I need to make more money. I need to buy more things. I need to work harder to get even more money.

"I see a wad of cash!"—Perry, 12

There's no time to sleep, eat, or smell the roses. I need money to pay for everything I just bought and am about to buy." Benjamin Franklin, one of our founding fathers, said, "Moderation in all things." What do you think that means?

Imagine you are at a big buffet. Food is piled up in trays all down the long table. Rather than pig out, the best thing to do is to take a little bit of several things you think you will like. Eat slowly, and enjoy the tastes. If you can resist going back for more, good for you. If chicken wings or cheese sticks are among the yummy delights, it may be very hard to pass up a second helping, but that's moderation.

"I see green. Lots of green."—Tim, 17

30

A person with money smarts...

- doesn't keep giving in to the little voice in his head that screams, "I want it now!"
- is happy with what he or she has.
- is not unhappy because of what he or she doesn't have.
- knows how to make money work for him or her.
- is usually careful and precise with money.
- does not waste things.

"I see clothes on a giant sales rack."—Ali, 12

Wasteful and careless people are often not too swift with money!

Chapter Three
MAKING IT

Depending on how old you are, your income will probably be more or less limited. Still, there will be times when you'll have some money coming in, and have a chance to make more. For most kids, their big source of income is something called allowance.

ALLOWANCE—THE BIG A

Allowance is money that some kids get on a regular basis from their parents or a guardian. The idea behind it is to give them practice spending, saving, sharing, and keeping track of their own money. The money you get in allowance is supposed to make you think about how much things cost, so you will learn to make smart money decisions. It also teaches you to appreciate the items that you are able to buy.

If you get an allowance, you have a chance to show how responsible you are with money. If your parents have said no, try to respect their decision. Remember that there are ways to earn money, as you'll see in the next chapter. And, when you start showing you are money-smart, your parents may notice and reconsider the allowance.

CHORES OR NOT

Lots of families link allowance to chores. Kids may get an agreed-upon amount of money each week as payment for setting the table, emptying the dishwasher, making the beds, or taking out the trash. If you don't do your chores, you may not get your allowance.

There are also some families who believe that allowance should not be tied to chores. They believe that household chores are what you do as a member of the family, and you shouldn't be paid for something you are expected to do. The theory is that the grown-ups don't get an allowance for making dinner or doing the laundry, so why should the kids?

But many families agree that some chores, those that take up more time or effort, such as painting the fence, or cleaning out the attic, may call for a few extra bucks.

"When I first started getting an allowance, I had trouble sorting out the things I needed from the things I wanted. Once I got a little extra allowance to buy some clothes for school. I spent so much on the sneakers that I ran out of money to buy socks and underwear." —Nicki, 13

WHEN IS PAYDAY?

Some money experts believe that allowance should be distributed on a regular basis, on a set day, at a specific time, like Fridays at 4:00 p.m. After all, in the real world, people get paid at a set time. It's much easier to keep track of that way, too.

It's worth noting that when you spend your own money, you may be less willing to part with the big dollars. If it's coming from your pocket, you may decide to buy the cheaper sneakers so that you'll also be able to save a little cash. Or, you may find yourself taking better care of the stuff you buy. If you can keep something looking new, you won't have to replace it. That means more cash in your pocket.

HOW MUCH ALLOWANCE SHOULD YOU GET?

Some money experts suggest an allowance of a dollar a week for each year of your life. So, if you're nine, you would get nine dollars a week. Others believe it should depend on these factors:

● What your parents can afford. The amount has to meet their budget.
● How much other kids your age with similar needs are getting.
● Where you live. In places like New York or California, things usually cost more than they do in Iowa or Montana.

MANAGING ALLOWANCE

In a perfect world, allowance would be adjustable. It would increase as you got older, and it would also increase around the holidays, and at times during the year when you need to buy special things, such as school supplies, birthday presents, and things for vacation. But it's not a perfect world, and for many kids, allowance is not adjustable. So, it is up to you to plan ahead and save for those special items or occasions throughout the year.

"When planning out how you will spend your allowance money, don't forget to include stuff like taxes and bus fare."—Danny, 10

Expect to make a few mistakes with your money. You may find that one week, you've spent most of your allowance by midweek. When that happens, try to save more the following week. Don't be too hard on yourself if you've spent too much; remember, we learn from our mistakes.

Try to plan it out before they dole it out. Know how much you plan to save, spend, and share in the coming week. Planning ahead may eliminate unplanned spending.

Don't lose it. Keep your money in a safe place. Carrying it around with you all the time is not a good idea. If your money is not with you, in your pocket, you won't spend it.

ALLOWANCE DOS AND DON'TS

Dos

❶ Do be reasonable. If your parents tell you that they can't afford to give you an allowance, respect that and understand that they have budget constraints of their own. What other ways can you earn some money (see next chapter)?

❷ Do sit down with your parents and create the ground rules before money is exchanged. Will your allowance money cover school lunches? Friends' birthday presents? Charitable donations?

❸ Do establish with your parents a set time each week to get your allowance. (Tell them that's the way it is in the real world!)

❹ Do ask your parents for tips about budgeting your money.

❺ Do learn from your allowance mistakes.

❻ Do keep a record of where your money goes.

❼ Do plan your purchases before you go shopping.

❽ Do keep your allowance in a safe place.

❾ Do remember to include sales tax when planning out your purchases.

Don'ts

❶ Don't spend every penny of your allowance. Leave at least a little for savings and sharing.

❷ Don't fret if you blow some of your money; make a pact with yourself that next week you'll be smarter with it.

❸ Don't buy anything with your money until you've thought about it carefully.

❹ Don't be upset if your friends get more allowance than you; accept the challenge of trying to stretch your cash.

❺ Don't ask for a raise in allowance if you do a good job at school. Ask for a hug instead.

WHEN IT'S TIME TO ASK FOR A RAISE

Want a raise in your allowance? Here are some things to think about before you ask your parents for more allowance. Keep in mind that if you can do this well, it will serve as excellent practice for asking for a pay raise once you have a job.

❶ Prove to your parents that you are being responsible about money in general. Talk about how you have cut down on phone calls, are saving electricity costs by shutting off lights, always check to make sure water is not left running, etc.

❷ Offer to take on some new responsibilities around the house, either in return for the raise or just because you are eager to help out.

❸ Show your parents your weekly or monthly budget. Be organized. Explain how you've managed to increase savings, decrease spending.

❹ Remain calm. Don't get overemotional. A bad reaction from you can make things worse.

❺ Approach your parents when they are in a happy mood, not when they are in the midst of a heart-to-heart, sleeping, or watching a tearjerker.

SAVE IT!

Here are 14 quick-and-easy ways to save cash!

❶ Bring lunch to school at least three days a week.

❷ Make, don't buy, Halloween costumes. Use old clothes and items from around the house to craft something original.

❸ Swap dressy clothing with a friend.

❹ Check out secondhand stores. There's a lot of cool and cheap vintage stuff out there.

❺ Swap books with your friends or use the library. When you do buy books, buy only paperbacks.

❻ Share magazine subscriptions with siblings and friends.

❼ When going out to eat, order water instead of soda; it's free. Water will also save you calories and it's good for you for you.

❽ Attend free concerts in the park and other community events that are fun and don't cost money.

❾ Clip coupons for personal items you use, such as hair gel, body lotion, or nail polish.

❿ Wear your old stuff. Make it a policy to wear something at least 30 times before even thinking about buying something new. Style-it-up or accessorize for a different look.

⑪ Get together with friends to have a community tag sale. Combine your baby furniture, toys, clothes, and books.

⑫ Don't browse stores with wads of cash in your pockets. It could be very expensive.

⑬ Make your own stationery and holiday and birthday cards.

⑭ Don't buy snacks at the park or the mall. Bring them from home.

SMART MONEY TIPS

INSTANT SAVING

Ask your parents to give you five one-dollar bills instead of a five-dollar bill, or ten one-dollar bills instead of a ten-dollar bill. That way, you can immediately set aside a few dollars for saving and sharing.

PERFECT RECORDS

Keep a shoebox to hold sales receipts from stuff that you buy with your allowance. Store the box under your bed. If you need to return something, you'll have your receipt, and a record of your purchase.

CAN WORK "WORK" FOR YOU?

One day in the not-so-distant future, you will have to earn a living. (And you thought school was challenging!) You will join the work force in order to pay for what you need or want—maybe a boogie board, a cruise to Alaska, a Shetland pony, a handheld talking computer that tells you what to have for dinner, and all your other needs and wants.

Get an edge on the work world by getting a job now. What will you gain? You'll learn to deal with all sorts of people. You'll get a heads-up about managing money, and you could have a nice pile of cold, hard cash before you hit your teen years. (It's never too early to start saving for a car or college!)

Whether it's mowing lawns, baby-sitting, recycling cans, pet-sitting, or doing odd jobs for neighbors, young people today can definitely make a buck. And if you're really savvy, you can even become a successful entrepreneur (a person who has his/her own business). So, if you're too young for working papers, or if you don't yet have the means to take on a job waiting tables, or doling out ice cream, don't fret—there's a lot out there that you can do.

ARE YOU READY FOR A JOB?

How do you know when it's time to get a job? Ask yourself the questions below and select the answer that best describes how you feel.

❶ Do you find yourself with a little too much time on your hands?
   a. Yep. **b.** Nope, I can stare at the clock on the wall for hours.
❷ Do you wish you could meet new people?
   a. Yep. **b.** Nope, I don't really get along with people.
❸ Do you want to learn something, other than the words to your favorite commercials?
   a. Yep. **b.** Nope, silly jingles are my life.
❹ Would you like a little pocket money?
   a. Yep. **b.** Nope, who needs money, when you've got good looks?
❺ Do you spend your allowance like it's going out of style?
   a. Yep. **b.** Nope, I spend it before I get it.
❻ Are you tired of asking, make that "begging," for money?
   a. Yep. **b.** Nope, my parents need to get second jobs to support my video game habit!

Your Score
If you answered "yep" to three or more questions, it's time to get a job!

BE YOUR OWN BOSS

Make some money by starting and managing a business. A successful entrepreneur, pronounced ahn-treh-preh-NURR, is:

imaginative It takes a strong imagination to come up with a bold idea.

creative It takes a ton of creative juice to design something fresh and new.

energetic You need energy to start up a new business. It may take 25 tries.

determined You won't give up. There is a way to work it out, and you'll find it.

organized You keep excellent records and can stick to your budget.

Find a business here to match your skills. Try one or two or three.

Love tots?

If you have a way with little kids, be a baby-sitter. Parents are often willing to pay well for a friendly and reliable baby-sitter. Better yet, you and several friends can form a baby-sitting service. Create a flyer that includes your services, references, and availability. If you're too young to baby-sit on your own, be a parent's helper in the summer or after school. You can feed, play with, or read to a toddler while a parent does work around the house or cares for another child. By the time you're old enough to baby-sit on your own, you'll have some good contacts.

Tip Enhance your skills by taking a baby-sitting class at your local YMCA or Red Cross chapter. You may learn first-aid and safety tips that will come in handy when you're on the job.

Like to play with cars?

Team up with a few friends to provide a unique car-washing service. How about providing coffee, donuts, free newspapers, and music while customers wait for their car to be cleaned? The "special service" may cost a bit extra, but could make your business more unique and profitable in the long run. Remember, people who care about their cars need them washed at least once a month. Find out what a car wash goes for in your area and set your prices a little lower. If you do a good job, you'll have steady business all spring and summer.

Tip When working with others, divide the work into various jobs. One person can greet the customer, another can wet and rinse, another can vacuum, another can dry the windows, and another can take the money and give a receipt. Take turns, so that each person gets a chance to do each task.

Come to life in the company of animals?
Put your personality and your passion into the job. Earn daily dollars by walking, grooming, or watching animals. Send out flyers and offer new customers a discount coupon. Give your pet business a zippy name, like Monkey Biz, Furry Friends, or Dog Days.

Tip This is the kind of business that really takes off if customers trust and like you. Make your references available. Go the extra mile. Make a daily report that includes details about what the pet did that day and give it to the customer. If you are grooming a dog, be sure not to leave a wet mess and, for a special touch, tie a bright ribbon around the dog's neck.

Outdoors is where you want to be?
Lawn care is still one of the best ways for young people to make money. You can offer a complete line of services including, mowing, weeding, trimming, and

flower maintenance. Work with a small group of friends, make it a goal to get a new customer every week, and always leave the yard neat and tidy.

Tip *Type up your prices and let the customer know exactly what you expect to be paid before you start to work.*

Chef in the making?

Go beyond the lemonade stand—how about an outdoor cafe? Offer herbal iced teas, soft drinks, and gourmet lemonade (lemonade poured over a cup of crushed ice). Add a variety of neatly bagged snacks. Set your refreshments on a wagon or cart. Post a menu with prices. Use coolers filled with ice to keep refreshments cold. Get permission to set up at tag sales and other community events, or near a playground, tennis court, or pool. Hang a bright and colorful sign with an arrow pointing toward your stand. Good prices and the right location are key.

Tip *Offer free samples to tempt customers, bring lots of coins to make change, and dress up your refreshment stand with a colorful paper tablecloth.*

Handy with details?

Be on-hand help or a personal assistant for a day. You can offer to do anything from closet cleaning to shining shoes, to shopping, to repotting plants, to helping plan a party.

Tip *Make a list of all the services you can offer to give to your customers. Smile and take your work seriously.*

Technology turns you on?

Create sensational mailers or personalized holiday cards or family newsletters.

Tip If you can type, design, and publish on the computer, present your customers with a folder of your samples. You can create signs, banners, personalized calendars, stationery, or offer a typing service. Charge by the page.

Good at arts and crafts?

Make your own picture frames, beaded jewelry, T-shirts, 3-D animal bookmarks (made from felt scraps and buttons), or sell personalized scrapbooks.

Tip When you present your design samples, have price lists and order forms handy. Take all your supply costs into account and the amount of profit you want to make per item before setting your prices.

Make 'em laugh?

Be the entertainment at birthday parties for toddlers. Wear a costume. Many popular characters come in kid-sized costumes. Invest in a face-painting kit. Make sure to have some favorite children's books on hand. If there's a lull in the party, you can share a favorite story.

Tip When working with young children, have a bunch of ideas up your sleeve, clean up as you go, and always make sure that safety is your biggest concern.

Weathered a storm?

If you live in a snowy climate, cash in on it! Team up with a pal, invest in a few shovels, and clear driveways and sidewalks of snow. Lots of snow could mean lots of dough!

Tip Make arrangements with your regular customers to shovel snow after every snowfall.

FIRST THINGS FIRST

Before your business blasts off, always make sure that:

- you are safe. Make sure your parents know where you are at all times. Also make sure you are comfortable with the job you are doing, and that you have all the information you need to complete the task. Never sell door-to-door by yourself. Trust your instincts; if something doesn't feel right, don't do it.

- you've worked out exactly how much money you need to start up your business. Have a plan. Where is the money coming from to buy the supplies? How much money do you want to earn? Will you be able to make a profit?

- you learn as much as possible about the job you are doing. If you are taking care of dogs, you'd better know about dogs. If you are going to do lawn work, you need to know how to weed and trim. If you are going to sell gourmet snacks, select several tried and true recipes that are easy to prepare.

44

- you like what you do. If you are miserable doing the job you've chosen, it's probably not the job for you. Find something that you enjoy doing and can do well.
- it fits your schedule. School comes before your business; so does basketball practice and violin lessons. Make sure to check your calendar and allow yourself plenty of time to complete your jobs.
- it stays your job, not someone else's. If the job you've set for yourself becomes too much for you, don't pass it off to Mom or Dad. That's just not right.
- you are fair with prices. When setting up prices for your goods, total up the cost of all your materials and add something for time and labor. You will want to cover all your expenses, plus make a little profit. If you are setting an hourly rate for a service, find out what other kids are charging for similar jobs.
- you act like a professional. Be on time, greet your customers with a smile, treat them well, and do your work responsibly.

Finally, always remember to:
- make time for work and play.
- ask a parent or grown-up for advice or help if you need it.
- put some profit back into the business.

WARNING!

If you take a job, be serious about it. It's a big responsibility. You may need to keep track of the hours that you will be expected to work. You may need to make sure that you have a ride to and from the job. And you'll have to make a commitment to do the best job possible. You do that for yourself, as well as your customers.

PUT YOUR BEST FOOT FORWARD

10 ways to increase your earning power

1 Read the newspaper. If you know what's going on in the world, you'll be able to talk to people. Everyone will know that you are a smart person with ideas.

② Practice the art of casual conversation. You don't have to go up to total strangers and ask them how they are, but get in the habit of saying hello and how are you to the people in your path.

③ Always put your best foot forward. If you have an interview for a job, or if you are meeting your aunt Lucy's boss, look neat and clean. Beware of dirty fingernails!

④ Be an eye-contact sort of a kid. Always look people in the eye when you talk to them. This puts them at ease, lets them know you're sincere and trustworthy.

⑤ Negotiate. If somebody offers you a job and the pay doesn't sound quite right to you, or the hours are long, don't just accept the deal. Try to get the best arrangement for yourself. After all, you're worth it.

⑥ Sell yourself. Know your strong points. Know your weak points. Write them down. Are you good with a scooter, a frying pan, and a calculator? Could you use more help in science and playing basketball? Be prepared to talk about your strong points. Learn to put your weak points in a positive way. For example, "When it comes to math, there's lots of room for improvement; however, I excel in sports and English."

⑦ Be interesting. Talk about your personal experiences and mention several things that you like to do for fun. Ask your customer what he or she enjoys.

⑧ Stand tall. No slouching. Good posture is key.

⑨ Watch your body language. Keep your hands out of your pockets, and don't look bored or tired. Smiling is good.

⑩ Keep your sense of humor at all times. That helps to put others at ease and makes any awkward situation a lot easier to deal with.

FUTURE FORTUNE

Work. It may be a four-letter word, but that doesn't mean it can't be awesome. Love what you do. Do it for the love of it. What interests and skills can you polish now to prepare for your future career? Here are some ideas:

Is music your passion?

Is your idea of fun playing karaoke, or singing into your hairbrush? Are you fascinated by music videos? If you can sing or play an instrument, be a musical performer. If you prefer to be behind-the-scenes, consider managing or promoting a band, or getting involved in music video production.

Do you love building things?

Are you into designing skyscrapers and using blocks to create bridges and play-grounds? If you are good at measuring, planning, and using numbers, you might be meant to be an architect or a contractor.

Are you a big talker?

Do you dream of using your language skills to find the job of your dreams? If you like to ask questions, consider becoming a reporter. Or how about a publicist, a speechwriter, or a newscaster?

Do you love words?

Are you an avid reader? Do you collect books? How about becoming an editor, a writer, a bookstore manager, or a librarian?

Are you a techie at heart?

Would you like to design software, create a cool state-of-the-art computer or cell phone? Why not start up your own technology company or go out and work for one of the big companies?

Do you live for sports?

If you like to play, try to pursue your dream to be a professional athlete. If you love to be around sports and athletes, be a sports writer or radio or tv game announcer.

Do you dream of putting out fires or stopping crime?

Do you like to help and protect people? Are you strong, committed to the idea of hard work, and not afraid to defend others? Become a police officer or a firefighter.

Do health and fitness interest you?

Do you want to unlock the mysteries of the body? Do you want to find a cure for cancer or AIDS? Consider becoming a doctor, a nurse, a wellness expert, or a yoga instructor.

Are you "teacher" when you play with your friends or siblings?

Maybe that's something that you would like to do in real life—mold minds by becoming a teacher.

Do you like to sell things?

Go into marketing or advertising, or be a sales representative and sell a product that you believe in.

Do you like to cook?

Does mixing, stirring, and creating yummy things make you happy? Be a chef. Combine all your skills to create your own food business—a restaurant, a cooking show, a product such as fat-free brownies. Cooking combines all your talents and you'd like to make a living out of it.

Earnings are not the only measuring stick when it comes to personal success. Make no mistake, money is important. It pays the bills. But there are lots of other things to think about when it comes to making a living—personal satisfaction, challenge, and happiness.

Chapter Four
USING YOUR MONEY SMARTS

Now let's use what we've learned to get and keep control of our money. Between spending it and getting an allowance or bringing money in, it's all in your hands. And money is not always easy to hold on to. How can you manage your income and spending?

DID YOU SAY BUDGET?

How much money do you spend every month on video games or CDs? How about special treats at the mall, or snacks at school? What if you didn't spend that money, but saved it for two or three months? Suddenly you'd have a stash for something special! But how can you stop yourself from spending? By making and sticking to a budget.

A budget is a plan that helps you keep track of your money. It lets you know how much comes in (income) and where all that money goes (the candy store, the bank, the movies) so you can control your spending. With practice, making a budget and sticking to it is easy. Soon you'll wish you had started a long time ago, before you frittered away all that cash! But there's no time like the present. And budgeting can be a fun and rewarding challenge, especially if you set yourself realistic money goals.

The first step in setting up a budget is to find out exactly where you are right now. You do this by making a list of your income—where your money comes from every week.

My Budget

Average weekly income:

Allowance	$15.00
Lunch money	$12.00
Odd jobs	$22.00

Next, list your weekly expenses. Balancing your budget means subtracting your expenses from your total income. If you get a negative number you are spending too much. You are over budget! You need to get back on budget by either increasing your income or decreasing your expenses.

Average weekly expenses:

School lunch	$10.00
Snacks	$6.00
Clothes/accessories	$12.00
Entertainment (videos, movies, books, magazines)	$10.00
Drugstore & misc. spending	$5.00
Total	$43.00

$49.00 – $43.00 = $6.00 for saving, sharing, investing

Now that you have figured out where your money is going, you can look for ways to cut back on spending. For example, do you really need to be spending an average of $10.00 each week on entertainment? Why not swap books and videos with friends? Could you bring your lunch from home at least two days a week for more savings?

Budgeting does not have to be painful. The trick is to find a formula that's right for you and your personality type. Do you prefer doing things on a weekly basis? Or would a monthly budget be better for you? Do you like to keep track of things on the computer or by hand? Do you carry around a small notebook, so you can easily jot down expenses? Do you save receipts and add up exact amounts, or round off expenses according to memory? Remember, saving money means learning to live on less than what you have. Sometimes you need to be inventive in coming up with new ways to trim the fat from your expenses.

THE FAMILY BUDGET

Does your family have a budget? What kind of expenses are involved in running a house? Ask your parents if they will show you their monthly budget. Can you offer any smart money-saving ideas? To save money, how about suggesting that your family buy some items, such as paper goods or dry cereal, in bulk?

Keep copies of your weekly budgets. There's a lot you can learn from them. Study them to see where you might be able to decrease expenses. Budgeting, like other important tasks, gets easier with time and experience.

How much do you think you spend each month on snacks? Movies? Clothes? Write down everything you spend for a month. See how it all adds up? Where could you possibly cut back?

MONEY JAMS

For every problem there is usually a solution, maybe even several solutions. Here are some scenarios to rev up your brain as a problem-solver:

The Problem

I'm too impatient to save money. I keep setting aside half of my allowance each week to save for a drum set. But by midweek I get so tired of waiting to have enough money that I blow a few bucks on snacks and junk. Then I am even more behind in my savings plan. I just can't seem to break the pattern.

A Solution

Sounds like you may be being too hard on yourself. Give yourself a little flexibility when it comes to how much you save each week. Is it really realistic to set aside half of your allowance for savings? Set aside a few dollars each month for miscellaneous items, like a candy bar, a frozen yogurt, or a root beer float. It may take you a little longer to save for your drum set, but this way, you can at least enjoy life while you're saving.

The Problem

I like trendy stuff. I want whatever is new and hip. I know that I am wasting a lot of money, because what's in now is never in in a few months. But I am still a sucker for the latest trendy looks.

A Solution

Limit yourself to one trendy item every other month. Being trendy can be expensive. If you are a true trendy person, be a trendsetter—sew cool fabric patches on your jeans, make awesome bags out of colored felt. Turn items you already own into fashion statements. That's called being trendy on a budget.

The Problem

I have a close friend who always has a lot of cash. Every time we go somewhere and I am short on cash, he offers to pay for me. I have agreed to borrow the money a few times. I don't think my parents would want me borrowing money from anyone. I am too embarrassed to really tell my friend that I can't afford his friendship. What should I do?

A Solution

Some people who have a lot of money have no idea what it's like not to have a lot of money. That's why you have to let your situation be known. Come clean to your parents. Ask them if you can borrow the money to pay back your friend. Then, explain to your close friend that money is tight. Encourage your friend to spend time with you doing things that don't require huge gobs of cash—hang out in the park, on the basketball court, or at the local library. You get the idea.

The Problem

My best friend and I have the same birthday! We exchanged birthday gifts. She spent $5 on my gift and I spent $20 on hers. Now we both feel awkward.

A Solution

Don't let this birthday mishap strain your friendship. Laugh it off. Next year, set a dollar limit on the amount that you will spend for birthday presents or take each other out for pizza or ice cream sundaes.

The Problem

I am really into saving money. When I do spend, I like to make an educated purchase. I never buy anything without research. How much does the item cost? Where else can I buy it? Is there any way I can get it cheaper? It's a real challenge for me, but my friends make fun of me all the time. They think I am cheap and that I should just buy what I want without thinking about it.

A Solution

Get your friends interested in comparison shopping by letting them know how much money you've saved from all your research. Offer to help them comparison shop with their next purchase. They'll thank you for it in the end because wasting money is not cool.

SPEND, SPEND, THEN SPEND MORE, PLEASE!

Welcome to the consumer culture. You know, gotta have it now, gotta get the best one, the deluxe model, the top of the line. Young people spend billions of dollars each year on food, CDs, clothing, movie tickets, books, and games.

It's great to be a consumer, but when you're buying, look for quality, and try not to overspend. Overspending is that trap that you sometimes fall into when your eyes are bigger than your wallet.

ADVERTISING IS NOT WHAT IT APPEARS

If you're like most kids, you've spent a lot of time watching TV. By now, you've probably absorbed some 30,000 television commercials. That's a lot of powerful messages about candy, cereal, fast-food treats, and toys. And, if you're like many kids, you may believe that crunchy candy can make you popular and happy, the doll will grant you instant friends, or the cereal will make you super strong and smart.

But when was the last time you bought something based on a promise from a TV commercial? Did the product live up to its promise?

Just because we see something advertised on television, it doesn't mean the product is really the best. It just means that some people paid a lot of money to get airtime for their product.

Advertisers are seeking you out. They want you to spend all your money on their products. And advertisements are not just on television. Beware of ads on the Internet, on roadside billboards, on the backs of products such as cereal boxes, in magazines, on radio, and those company logos on our clothes.

IMMEDIATE GRATIFICATION BLASTER

Try to resist that voice inside of you! Those jeans you've just decided to buy. The beaded choker you absolutely have to own. The sneakers. (That's your third pair this year!) The DVD player. The rollerblades. All things you want. You may even think you need them. And maybe you do. And maybe you don't. You'll never know until you get with the Immediate Gratification Blaster program.

Immediate gratification, the need to have it now, is at the heart of an over-spender's problem. An over-spender might see something and not take the time to think about the purchase. Your inner voice tells you, "I want it now!"

Next time you find yourself face-to-face with the hottest fashion accessory since the temporary tattoo, or yearning to bite into a fancy wrap sandwich that costs three times the price of a sandwich that you can make at home, give it the IGB test.

The IGB Test

Step One

Drop it. Let go of the item. Release it. Keep blinking your eyes to erase the item from your vision. Then, stick a mental picture of the item in the window of your imagination (in your head).

Step Two

Step away from the item. Change your perspective. Mentally flick the lights in the room. Open the shade and take a fresh look. Is it still there? Do you still want it? Has something changed?

Step Three

Transform yourself into the person you know with the best money smarts. Is it a parent, a relative, a neighbor, or a friend? Now really look at your mental picture as that person. Would that person want or need to buy that? Would that person think that buying that item would be a smart and savvy purchase?

Step Four

You must really want this thing because you've made it to step four. Now take out your mental image and talk to it. Tell it what you're expecting from it. Are you hoping to look cool because of it? Or may seem a little smarter with it? Tell it what you want from it. Now, when you spoke to it, did it talk back to you? If it did, if it really talked to you, then go buy it already!

TIME TO SHOP

Imagine you are in your favorite clothing store. You are shopping for fall clothes for school, but a big sale sign catches your attention. It turns out all summer pants, shorts, and T-shirts are 75 percent off the regular price! That's a lot of savings. What will you do with your money? Spend it on fall clothes like you planned? Or, do you take the opportunity to save money by buying items you know you will be needing, even if not for two or three seasons? It may be hard to think of buying summer clothes when the leaves are turning and Halloween is just around the corner. But if you're a really thrifty shopper, you'll think ahead. End-of-season sales are a good time to stock up.

Buying things out of season to give as gifts can be a great money-saving idea. And nobody but you has to know when you actually bought the stuff.

IMPULSE BUYING

Many items that we buy are unplanned. In some grocery stores, customers may be tempted with free samples of yummy freshly-made goods—chocolate chip cookies, apple cider, blueberry pie, and other gourmet treats. A shopper who plans on just buying milk, eggs, and butter may fill his cart with dozens of other unplanned but delicious items. Impulse buying is not a bad thing unless it gets out of control. If you are going to the supermarket for a quart of milk, and you're returning with everything but the kitchen sink, you may need to stay out of those stores!

WHERE TO BUY

Shopping today can mean a trip to a huge mall or a visit to a specialty or outlet store. Or, it can mean a virtual trip to an on-line store. Shopping can also mean sitting in your living room with a mail-order catalog in your lap. There are so many shopping alternatives.

Department stores are ideal for buying clothing, gifts, jewelry, and housewares. These stores are known for their service. If you need to return or exchange merchandise, department stores are your best bet. Department store salespeople are usually helpful, and may even give you a heads-up about when an item is going on sale.

Specialty stores, often small and locally owned, are generally more expensive than department stores or discount stores. But here's where you may find original and funky stuff, like sweaters with faux fur trim, or silk scarves. If you have cool and unusual taste, you may get some great buys here. Especially if you believe that less is more.

Discount stores offer great bargains, but you may have to sort through some junk.

Outlet stores offer good shopping values. But often the merchandise is less than perfect, or is left over from a previous season. Make sure to examine the merchandise carefully before you buy something from an outlet store. You don't want to wind up with damaged goods that are not refundable. A lot of merchandise may be opened and soiled or broken.

On-line shopping lets you buy everything from fine candy to daffodils to cool sneakers for extra-wide feet. With a few clicks of your mouse, you can buy almost everything. But, when shopping on-line:

- have a parent or an adult make sure that you are on a secure site.
- review the site's privacy statement before you purchase anything.

- print out the receipt and confirmation. This will serve as a record in case you have a problem with your order.
- keep a record of the Internet address so that you can find them if you want to order something else, or if you have a problem.

> When I go shopping, I carry just enough money to pay for what I came to buy. That way I don't end up spending more money than I planned.—John, 13

Mail-order shopping offers great out-of-season and overstocked sales. It comes in handy around holiday time when you need to buy a lot of gifts.

Vintage shops are proof that some things truly are better the second time around. You can furnish a room with really unique stuff, or accessorize yourself with cheap retro stuff.

> Before I buy something, I compare the price of it in at least three different stores. That way I know I'm getting the best price.
> —Dani, 9

Secondhand is a great way to go when you are looking for clothing, shoes, costume jewelry, or decorative items. Be careful when you buy electronic items or sports gear second hand. Ask about a return policy before you buy.

Finally be a smart consumer. Comparison shop. Compare different brands of products. Talk to friends and relatives before you buy. Find out what brands they are most satisfied with. Research the product in the library (*Consumer Reports Magazine*). Go to several different stores before making the purchase. Use coupons to save money on food and other items. Clipping coupons may be time consuming, but it's time well spent.

> "I don't carry a lot of cash."—Lisa, 17

MONEY MISTAKES

You bought something. You just had to have it. But was it a mistake? If you bought it for any of the following reasons, you may have made a mistake:

- I bought it because I just felt like buying something.
- I bought it to be cool.
- I bought it because I've always wanted something like it for as long as I can remember.
- I bought it because I saw a commercial for it on TV so I had to have it.
- I bought it because everybody I know has one.
- I bought it to make me better looking.
- I bought it because I thought it would make me look smarter.
- I bought it because it was on sale.
- I bought it so people would like me better.
- I bought it because I thought it would make my life easier.

Okay, so you bought it and it was a mistake. What do you do now?

Don't sweat it. If the object doesn't work, doesn't fit, or just doesn't satisfy you, consider taking it back. You will need your receipt.

Learn from the experience and use it to help you gain instant willpower in the future. Next time you are about to buy something that you are not quite sure about, remember this experience.

Give it away to someone who will use it.

Sell it at your annual tag sale.

Chapter Five
GROWING IT

$\int$aving money can put a big smile on your face. There's a real sense of accomplishment when you set a money goal and reach it. You feel independent and smart when you can enter a store and buy something on your own, with money that you have saved up. Imagine how you feel when you exercise, eat right, write a story or poem, or do something that you know is right and good for your mind and body. You come to realize that you do have the discipline, willpower, and ability to do something well. It's the same feeling when you save up a stash of cash.

Here are five good reasons to save your money:
1. It may help make your dreams come true.
2. It may get you or someone you care about out of an unexpected jam.
3. It may give you the freedom to choose your own path and make choices.
4. It may keep you safe from certain dangers.
5. It can help you make a positive difference in the world.

Try This For the next two months, drop any spare change you find in your pockets at the end of the day into a glass jar. Watch it grow. At the end of the two months, count the change. Then do something special with it—donate it to a good cause, put it in the bank, or set it aside for holiday gifts. That's money you never even knew you had!

BANK ON IT!

Saving money means you'll have it if you need it for something you didn't plan for—if your speed bike needs repair, or you lose your eyeglasses and need new ones. And then there are those things that you need or want, but they are expensive enough to have to save for—a pair of skis, a new bedroom set, your own car. The best way to be sure you have money for such things is by saving your money in the bank, where it's safe and where you are less likely to just fritter it away.

EARNING INTEREST

Josie saves her baby-sitting money in an old shoebox. She likes to keep a close eye on it. Every once in a while she likes to give the box a shake. But how could Josie make her money grow? By depositing it in the bank in a savings account, where it would earn interest.

How does interest work? Suppose you put $100 in the bank and the bank agrees to pay you 5% interest each year. That means that the bank will pay you 5 cents on every dollar each year. After the first year, you will have earned $5 in interest.

When your money is in the bank, it's safe. The bank has fireproof steel vaults that can only be opened by bank staff under tight security regulations. When you deposit your money in a bank account, it lends the money out to someone else at a higher rate of interest than the bank is paying you. That's how the bank makes money. The bank pays you interest. That's how you make money. You can see the amount of money you get in interest when you get a bank statement or, if you have a passbook account, you go to the bank and have the interest posted. The money doesn't just sit there—it grows!

What if you cut out the middleman, the bank, and simply loaned your money to a friend and charged interest? How does that sound? Aha, but forget the interest, what if your friend doesn't even pay you back? You'd be out everything, even the friend. Sometimes borrowing and lending money sounds like a good idea, but it's always safer to do it officially, from a bank.

In the bank, the more money you have in a savings account, the more interest you earn. Many banks offer compound interest. That's better than just regular interest because you earn interest not only on your savings, but also on the interest you make on your savings. It gives you interest on your interest. Not bad!

Banks also offer special accounts called certificates of deposit, or CDs. These bank CDs can be music to your ears if you have saved a good amount of money, maybe toward your college education, and won't be needing it for awhile. The CDs pay higher interest rates the longer you leave the money in the account—but if you need to take it out sooner, you will be charged a penalty fee.

So, check out the banks in your area. See what they offer. Here are some questions to ask while shopping for the right bank:
- How much interest will I earn on my savings?
- Do I get a passbook to keep, or will I get bank statements?
- How often can I come in and have the interest posted?
- Is my money insured (in case of fire, flood, or robbery)?
- Do I need to keep a minimum amount of money in the account?
- Will I be charged a monthly fee if I don't keep a minimum balance?
- Will I be charged fees for other banking services?
- Does a free ATM card come with this account?

- Do I need a parent or adult on the account with me to get an ATM card?
- Do I need to keep the money in the account for a certain time period?
- What are your current interest rates for CDs (for different lengths of time)?

CHECK FOR CHECKING

The checkbooks that you get from banks are written promises that mean "I will pay." Having a checking account means that you don't have to carry wads of cash around with you. You can pay what you need to by just writing out a check. Of course, you have to have the money in your account to cover the checks. If the money is not there in your account and you "bounce" a check, you will have to pay a penalty.

Having a checking account means your money is safe. Checkbooks can be replaced if they are lost or stolen (but the bank does need to be notified in writing as soon as any such loss is discovered). Cash cannot be replaced. It is just gone—and that's not a good feeling!

If you qualify as a checking account customer (you probably need be 18 years old or older), you would get a statement every month. The statement would list all the checks that you have written that have cleared the bank (have been paid), each deposit you made, and charges for certain of the bank's services. One drawback is that checking accounts don't pay as much interest as savings accounts. There are often other fees when using checks, so if you just want to save money—not spend it—a savings account is the way to go.

PERSONAL BANKING

Be organized. Write down your account number(s) and who helped you open the account. Make a copy and put it in a safe place. Keep all your financial records in order, so you can find things if you need to. Loose-leaf or pocket folders are good for keeping monthly statements after you read them. Put copies of bank deposits and sales receipts for things you've bought—in case you need to return them—in labeled shoeboxes. Keep track of any payments made on large items and smaller loans that you have repaid—it's a good start on your credit history.

Best Places to Keep Your Money

Ready for a little quiz? In the following situations, which place— **a)** a bank **b)** a piggy bank **c)** your wallet —is the best place to keep your money?

1. When you are going to a store where the jacket you want is 50% off.
2. When all you can manage to save from your allowance each week is small change.
3. When you are looking for a special birthday gift.
4. When you are saving a part of your allowance for something that costs a lot.
5. When you are meeting someone you owe money to.
6. When your piggy bank is full.
7. When your allowance money just goes through your hands like water.
8. When you are treating a friend to the movies.
9. When you empty your pockets at night.
10. When you win $100 in an essay contest.

Answers:
1. c **2.** b **3.** c **4.** a **5.** c **6.** a **7.** a **8.** c **9.** b **10.** a

DO YOU ATM?

ATM (automated-teller machine) cards let you access money from your account at ATM machines. This is helpful for people who need money on weekends, on holidays, or in the evenings, when banks are usually closed. If you are old enough, or have a joint account with a parent or adult, you can get an ATM card when you open a savings account. Bank cards also come with checking accounts. To use an ATM card, you will have to pick a Personal Identification Number (called a PIN). This four-number code will be the code you enter into the ATM machine each time you use your card. This prevents someone else from using your card if it is lost or stolen. You will need to remember your PIN or keep it in a safe place—but not with the card!

ATM cards are not always the cheapest way to get to your money. Watch out for annual fees that every ATM cardholder must pay. Also, there may be a fee to pay each time you use your ATM card—there will be if you use an ATM not connected to your bank. Those fees can really add up—sometimes you pay a double fee, one by the ATM's bank and one by your own! So before you whip that card out at the sight of any ATM, consider the fees you'll be paying. Should your card be stolen or if it gets lost, call the bank right away. And remember: Never, ever give your PIN to anyone!

YOUR ASSETS

You may or may not have a lot of cash, but you may have other things, given to you or inherited from members of your family, that could be worth a lot of money.

Most people, at some time in their lives, collect things. Some happily collect rocks and driftwood from trips to beaches and treasure the memories they bring. Others collect certain items that interest them, and may appreciate, or increase in value, over time such as coins, stamps, antiques, baseball cards, paintings and sculptures, jewelry, fine china, or rare books. Sometimes, rather than sell such collections, older family members may pass individual pieces or prized possessions on to young people they favor and who they think might enjoy or appreciate them.

Some items worth a good bit of money sometimes find their way into thrift stores, flea markets, and garage sales and can be picked up for a few cents. But that doesn't mean you should run right out and buy everything you see there. Like baseball cards, some can be worth a lot, and some aren't worth the cost of the gum.

INVESTING 101

Investing means putting your money to work in the hope that it will make you more money. The sooner you start investing your money, the more time it will have to grow. The more time your money has to grow, the better off you'll be.

There are many ways to invest money. The most common ways are in a savings bank where your money will earn interest, and in bonds, stocks, and mutual funds. We already know that banks pay us interest for keeping our money in a savings account, but how do bonds, stocks, and mutual funds work?

Bonds

Bonds are loans to companies or governments. The company or government promises to pay you back by a certain date and also gives you interest on your money—your loan. Many people give these bonds, usually government savings bonds, as gifts to newborn babies or as birthday presents to kids. By buying the bonds, they feel they are lending money to help the country grow, and the bond appreciates, is worth more, as the child grows up. The dollar amount that is paid for the bond is called the principal. The amount of interest that the bond pays is usually determined by the strength of the government or company to pay back the principal plus the interest rate promised. United States government and savings bonds are considered very safe, but bonds from newly formed companies or troubled countries may be considered much more risky.

Stock

A stock is a small piece, or share, of a company. People who own stocks are called shareholders. If you buy stock in a company and want your money back, you have to sell your stock. If you do sell your stock and the price is higher than when you bought it, you make money, and it could be a lot. But if the price of the stock is lower than when you bought it, you will lose money if you sell it. Stock prices go up and down all the time.

People who buy shares of a company do so for two reasons: dividends and value.

Dividends — As the company makes money, some of that money is paid out in dividends. Dividends are earnings based on the percentage of each share that you own. The more shares you own, the more money you make.

Value — When a company grows, the value of the stock increases. The more valuable the company becomes, the higher the stock price goes.

Mutual funds are lots of different stocks or bonds grouped together. When you buy shares in a mutual fund, you and many others own a very small part of the whole fund collection. A fund manager decides which stocks, bonds, and other investments to buy with the money collected from investors. By investing in a mutual fund, you can own stocks in several different industries—technology, medicine, international companies, or companies that protect the environment.

SIX THINGS TO KNOW

If you're thinking of investing your money:

1. You will have to ask a parent or guardian to make your investments for you because you are a minor. In order to buy stock, you must be at least 18 years old. You will need to open an account with a stockbroker, who will do the buying and selling for you. Accounts are opened in person, by mail, by phone, or on the Internet.

2. Your goal as an investor is to build an increasingly larger and more profitable portfolio, a collection of investments.

3. There are all kinds of investments with all kinds of risks. Some investments are very high-risk. That means you may make a lot of money, but you also may lose a lot of money. There are also investments that are considered low-risk,

and almost no-risk. How you invest your money depends on your personality, your appetite for adventure, and what is happening in your life.

❹ Ask questions about the investment you're considering: What if I end up with less money than I started with? How soon can I get my money if I need it? How can I find out more about the particular investment?

❺ Know the risks involved and try to match your personality to the right level of investment risk. If you like life in the fast lane, and you can afford to lose the money, go for it. But if you worry about losing your money, do something more conservative. Of course, less risk may mean less profit on your money.

❻ Don't put all your eggs in one basket. That means, try to diversify; put money into several different kinds of investments, not just in one. That way, if you take a loss on something, chances are you'll make a profit on something else.

WHAT KIND OF INVESTOR WILL YOU BE?

Are you a high-risk, medium-risk, or low-risk personality? Do you enjoy taking big chances, or do you run from risks? If there's a 50% chance of rain in the forecast, do you take your umbrella and rain gear, or do you risk it? Find out about your risk level with this quiz. Which of the responses below best reflects your personality.

❶ You have been selected to study abroad for a year. It's a great opportunity to learn, meet new people, and see the sights. You...
  a. are packed and set to go.
  b. are considering the trip, but you have a few second thoughts, like what will you do when you're homesick?
  c. could never be away from your family for so long.

❷ A new restaurant has just opened in your town and everyone is raving about the exotic daily specials. Today's special is poached ostrich with sun-dried tomatoes and plum sauce. You...
  a. go for it. Bon appetit!

b. are not quite willing to order the ostrich, but you agree to taste your friend's.

c. stick with something you know you like—the burger and fries.

③ You and your family have just won a free trip to a gorgeous island near Hawaii. Only catch is, there's a 1 in 600 chance that a giant volcano will erupt on that island while you are there. You...

a. go for it. Chances are, you'll be safe and sound.

b. go, but make sure to take precautions and keep your head up for volcanic activity.

c. plead with your parents to make new vacation plans.

④ You're at a brand-new state-of-the-art amusement park. The Rocking Rolling Coaster promises the ride of your life. You...

a. are first in line.

b. wait until your friends go on it to give you a report.

c. make a mad dash for the carousel.

⑤ As a contestant on the latest TV game show, you've just won $1,000. Now you have to decide whether to keep the money and stop the game, or trade the money in for what's behind the curtain. The prize could be a new computer, a check for $50,000, or a can of cat food. You...

a. go for the curtain.

b. ask for the input of the audience because you can't make up your mind.

c. keep the $1,000 and call yourself a big winner.

Your Score

For each **a** response, give yourself three points. For each **b** response, give yourself two points. For each **c** response, give yourself one point. Add up your score.

11–15 points ● Risky Frisky

Did someone say bungee jumping? Is "Go for it" your motto? Risk takers love thrills and adventure. As far as investing goes, risk takers are aggressive, jumping in where other investors fear to tread. You could make a lot of dough...or lose a lot. But that's fine with you, you love living dangerously.

6–10 points ● Middle of the Road

Every once in a while, taking a big chance—tasting something exotic, seeing a blood-tingling horror flick, riding a huge wave—may appeal to you. But mostly, you seek comfort with a medium amount of risk. That's what you tend to look for in your investments, too.

3–5 points ● Caution on the Sidelines
Your idea of taking a risk might be buying a raffle ticket. You like to know what's going to happen next. You don't like the idea of making a mistake. That makes you a conservative investor. You are looking for a sure bet.

THE STOCK MARKET

Think of a street or country fair, where people come with products to sell and others come wanting to buy. If a product is useful there will be many people interested in buying it. This will raise the price of that product. On the other hand, if a product does not work well, people will not be too anxious to buy it and, after a while, the price of that product will go down. That, in essence, is what the stock market is. It is a meeting place where buyers and sellers come together. Some will buy and some will sell.

In order for shares of stock to be traded, meaning bought and sold, there must be a buyer and a seller. But they don't talk face to face. Brokers arrange the trade. The broker for the buyer says how much the buyer is willing to pay for each share of the stock. The broker for the seller says how much the seller wants to receive. If the two brokers can agree on a price, the trade is made. Essentially, if you want to invest in the stock market, you aim to buy low, and sell high.

There are more than 140 exchanges all over the world. For example, there are stock markets in London, Paris, Hong Kong, and Tokyo. There are markets where only gold and precious metals are bought and sold. There are other markets that specialize in oil and gas, in rice and wheat, and in meat and soybeans.

Where the Trades Are Made

The New York Stock Exchange (NYSE), the largest organized stock exchange in the United States, started out as nothing more than a dirt path in front of a church in East New York 200 years ago. At that time, there was no paper money changing hands, and no stocks to buy. Silver, coming in on ships, was traded daily. In 1792, 24 men signed an agreement that established the NYSE.

Wall Street, the financial district, boomed in the early 1900s with the Industrial Revolution. Suddenly, the NYSE was not the only way to buy stocks. Some stocks that didn't make it onto the NYSE were traded outside on the curb. Formal rules and regulations transformed this open, outdoor "Curb Market" into an organized exchange and they moved indoors. In 1953, "The New York Curb Exchange" was renamed the American Stock Exchange (AMEX). The AMEX is the nation's second largest equities market and attracts and lists smaller companies than the NYSE.

The National Association of Securities Dealers Automated Quotation System

(NASDAQ) is different from the other two exchanges because it has no physical location. All trading is done on computer.

The Dow Jones Industrial Average (DJIA) is a daily measure of the overall performance of the stock market. The DJIA is the daily average of 30 stocks. If the average value of those stocks goes down, we say the stock has decreased. If the average value of those stocks goes up, we say the stock has increased.

Blue-chip stocks are the largest, most consistently profitable companies. The term comes from gambling. In poker, the most valuable plastic chips that are used instead of money are the blue chips. Some historical blue-chip stocks are: General Electric, IBM, and General Motors.

Finally, we get to the overall market—all the stocks taken together. Two animals represent the movement of stocks up or down. A bull market is an increase in stock prices, while a bear market is a decrease in stock prices.

Learning About Investing

Want to learn more about investing? Here's what you can do.

- Create an investment club and keep track of stocks. Use play money or have a parent sponsor you by making the investments for you.
- Watch the stock market closely. You and a friend can each select a stock to track. At the end of a month, determine who made the best investment. Who would have lost money? Make a graph to see how the stock climbed or fell.
- Instead of cash or clothes, let friends and family know that you are learning about investing and wouldn't mind bonds, stocks, and mutual funds as gifts.
- Start comparing stocks. Find a blue-chip company to learn more about. Request an annual report. What are the strengths and weaknesses of the company?
- Learn more about the stock market and the different companies represented from newspapers, television shows, the Internet, and company reports.

The Stock Report

To find the current value and other information on a stock, flip to the business section of a newspaper. Look for a listing of stocks in columns something like this:

	1		2	3	4	5	6	7	8
52-Wk									
Hi	Low		Symbol	Name	Div.	EPS	P/E	Last	Chg.
38	23		MM	Marlee Muffins	.10	.07	12	27.17	+.22

1 The highest and lowest prices of the stock over the past 52 weeks. This tells you how much the value of the stock has changed in a year—$38 was the high price per share, and $23 was the low price.
2 Sometimes the name, logo, or symbol for the company (usually 1 to 3 letters) is given. For example, here MM stands for Marlee's Muffins.
3 The company name—it may be shortened, but should be recognizable.
4 The dividend that some companies pay to shareholders. The dividend amount is the portion of the profits paid out per share.
5 The earnings per share. A company's EPS is the amount of profit the company made over the past year divided by the number of shares.
6 The price-to-earnings ratio. The P/E ratio comes from dividing the current price of a share by the earnings per share. A high P/E means investors are willing to pay top dollar for the stock.
7 The latest price of the stock, based on the last stock market session.
8 The amount of price change during the last session. In the case of MM, the company gained .22 cents. This may not seem like much, but if someone owns 100 shares of stock, they've just made $22.00.

CALLING ALL COLLECTORS

Stamps. Coins. Seashells. Dolls. Stickers. What do these things have in common?

They are all items that people collect. Whether it's perfume atomizers, postcards, autographs, stuffed animals, trading cards, or sports memorabilia, collecting can be a lifelong passion.

Some kinds of collections may increase in monetary value over time, but that should not be the sole reason for collecting. The most important thing, when you think of collecting, is to collect what you like. If you collect something just because it may be worth lots of money someday, you may not stick with it. And if you do, you may be sorry. Collecting may become a chore, and end up not worth whatever you finally get for it. So why do it? Collect something you like, and if it makes money, too, it's a win-win situation!

Also, you'll need to consider the space you'll need for your collection. Stamps, coins, baseball cards, miniature owls, small fossils, or other small items are good ideas for collectors with a minimum of space. Especially if you won't be allowed to take over the entire house with your collection. (Your parents refuse to move out and make room!) Also, you'll enjoy your collection more if you can leave it out, to look at it now and then and show to friends, than if you have to hide it away. So think "enjoyment" first, and then "investment." Don't collect something just because you think it will appreciate in value over time, and may fund your college education or your first convertible. If it doesn't happen, you may have wasted a lot of your funds, and fun years, on a pile of stuff nobody wants.

COLLECTOR'S CORNER

If you are a born collector—some people will collect practically anything!—here are some ideas to put you on the right track:

- Include objects from all over the world, giving it an international flair.
- Don't try to cover too big a topic—try to specialize.
- Display or store your collection in an appropriate place—weatherproof.
- Make sure it's safe from the hands and paws of siblings and pets
- Be an educated collector. Delve into the history that surrounds your collection.
- Find ways to combine your hobbies with the things you collect. For instance, save Playbills or theater programs if you love the theater. Or, collect teapots or cup-and-saucer sets if you are a tea drinker.
- Be skeptical when companies use words like "limited edition" and "collectible" to sell their products. While some toys and "collectibles" may increase in value over time, many won't. Collect something because you like it, not because you think it may fund your college education.

Chapter Six
BE IN CONTROL

Credit cards offer a way to buy things without having cash in hand. They can really make life convenient. But we pay for this plastic luxury. Some people who may be light on money smarts may pay greatly. Many fall victim to the dangers of out-of-control credit card spending. Don't you be one of them.

TO YOUR CREDIT

"Attention, Young People!" Finance companies will be tracking you down. They may soon be sending you mail or trying to get you on the telephone. They will promise you low interest rates, gift incentives, free bonuses, and more to get you to order their credit card. (They can't send one unless they get your okay.) Actually, college-age kids are the number one target for credit card companies looking for fresh customers. Learn all you can now about how credit cards work so that, by the time you are college age, you will know how to use a credit card responsibly.

Some finance companies are even offering kids their own credit cards. Let's say you're going to boarding school, or you're taking a trip across country for the summer. You'll definitely need some money. Rather than cash, carrying a credit card may come in handy.

Credit cards don't usually come with a user's guide, but some finance companies are giving kids crucial information about savings, credit, and interest payments followed by a short quiz. If a kid doesn't pass the quiz, he can't qualify for the card. These finance companies believe that if they equip young people with basic money skills, there will be a lot more young and smart consumers out there.

Some finance companies are offering parents a way to send money to their kids over the Internet. Kids can access the money as they need it and parents can go on-line to monitor their child's spending. A kid can also get a credit card that's linked to her parents'. That just means that the credit card company issues an extra card to family members. The card is good as long as purchases against the card haven't gone over the credit limit. Since account statements go to the parents, a child can simply repay his or her parents for anything bought on the card. (Parents might also consider providing a responsible young person with a debit card. This would allow the kid to withdraw money from the family account as needed. Of course, parents will definitely want to monitor this activity closely!)

What's good about credit cards?

They are ideal when you are in a bind. You never know when you will find yourself in a situation that requires money fast. Let's say you are in a store and break an expensive glass bowl, and a sign nearby says, "You break it, you bought it!" Would you have the cash on you? Or, what if you had planned on buying tickets to the circus when it came to town next month. All of a sudden, it's next month, and you won't have the cash until the circus tent is packed up and off to the next town.

They are accepted all over the world. Whether you find yourself in Tahiti, Alaska, or Egypt, you can just whip out your card. And no need to worry about changing currency and searching out the right amount, the credit card company does all the calculating for you.

They protect you in case of theft. You don't have to worry about someone stealing your cash if you don't carry any. And what if your credit card is lost or stolen? Report it immediately and the card will be invalidated, then you will be issued a new one.

What's bad about credit cards?

You have to pay annual fees. For each credit card you own and use, you will be charged a fee.

You have to pay interest fees. You're only required to make a minimum payment each month, but unless you pay off the full amount of the bill when you get it, the outstanding balance collects interest. That can really pile up!

You can start spending more than you can actually afford. It sounds great to "Buy Now, Pay Later," but that kind of spending can result in major credit card debt.

HERE'S WHAT YOU NEED TO KNOW

Congratulations, you have just received your first credit card. Read these facts and remember them each time you say, "Charge it."

- Plastic money is not free money. Charge only what you know you can afford to pay back.

- Charges should be paid back as soon as possible. When bills aren't paid in full, the outstanding balance collects interest. You run the risk of having to pay charges that you cannot catch up to.
- If you lose your card, notify the card issuer immediately to avoid having to be responsible for charges that don't belong to you.
- If you move, remember to update your account statement promptly to avoid any late charges.
- Review your monthly statement carefully. Make sure you can identify all charges. It may not be likely, but credit card companies sometimes do make mistakes, and it's up to you to find them.
- Beware of credit card companies that offer big incentives for you to spend, spend, spend. Remember, credit card abuse is like other types of addiction. Once it starts, it's very difficult to stop. Habits are hard to change.
- Think of your future. Credit problems stay with you. Binge out on credit cards now and you may not be able to get a student loan, buy a car, or own a home. If a creditor isn't certain that you will pay back the loan, why should he or she loan you money?

THE GOLD IN GIVING

People give of their money, their time, or what they have because they want to make the world a better place. What can be more important or more satisfying than the knowledge that a donation you made is improving someone's life?

How much you give in donations depends a lot on how you look at money and how much you can afford to give. Some people try to tithe, meaning give ten percent of their earnings. But the choice is up to you. Everyone's financial situation is different.

Giving a little on a regular basis works well because it makes giving a habit—a part of your budget and a part of your life. You can choose to make a monthly, twice yearly, or yearly donation to a charity, or you may want to simply give loose change, when you have it, to a recognized charitable or cultural organization. Donations to charitable and other approved nonprofit organizations can be deducted from income taxes.

In addition to giving money, many organizations will appreciate your offer of a more personal helping hand.

BE A FUND-RAISER

If you don't have money of your own to spare, you and your friends may want to host a fund-raising event for the organization. Try any of these fun fund-raising ideas:

Do a bake sale

A group of friends, a supervising adult, and an afternoon in the kitchen can yield muffins, cookies, cakes, and pies that you can sell in the park, near a shopping mall, or in front of your local library. Let your customers know where the proceeds are going. Also, keep a big jar on hand for additional donations. As a nice thank-you, offer customers a recipe or two, written on small index cards.

Have a car wash

Ask your parents and your friends' parents to donate old towels, rags, sponges, and buckets. Post signs about your car wash several days before the event so customers can plan ahead. Ask for your parents' support, and again, make sure to let everyone know where the proceeds are going.

Try a tag sale

Ask a few families on your block or in your neighborhood if they will donate old toys, clothes, books, furniture, and other things to your cause. Ask your neighbors for their input when setting your prices. Again, make sure to let everyone know where the proceeds will go. Make sure to send those neighbors who contributed their belongings and their time thank-you notes. Turn your efforts into an annual event.

Involve the community

Ask the local store owners in your area to donate goods and services—a coupon for a manicure, dinner for two, a pair of running shoes—

and host an auction. An adult can help you with the event.

Have guests bid on each item. This is a great way to get the local stores in your area involved in your cause.

Sing and dance

Have you and your friends ever thought of putting on a variety show? Now's your chance. Ask a parent to be the director and the producer and put together a few acts. Ask permission to use a public space for your production. Charge admission and let your audience know where all the proceeds will be going.

GIVE WITH YOUR HEAD AND YOUR HEART

Before you give money to a specific charity, ask your parents to check out the organization. There are, unfortunately, some phony organizations out there. They don't do as much good for people as they should with the money they get. A good

part of what they take in may go right into their pockets, or in simply sending out more requests for donations. Beware, too, of charities that claim you or a family member has won a prize, but that they can only send information if you agree to make a donation.

Always ask for written information about the charity before you donate. Once you've identified the charity that you like, write or call to request its annual report. The report will summarize the organization's achievements, and will give you a detailed account of how it spends its money.

Young people from all over the world have worked in unique ways to raise money for many charities and help organizations, especially during emergencies. Young people can be very powerful, successful, and strong when they work together toward a common goal.

YOUR MONEY SENSE

Learning to manage money well takes time. It's not a skill that can be learned in a few hours. It takes practice. It takes discipline, perseverance, and consistency. It helps to have family and friends who can help support and encourage you in your smart money-making decisions.

Smart money-managing skills make you feel good. There is something very cool about being in control of your money and knowing that it is not controlling you. This is true for people of all ages. It is difficult to feel positive about yourself and the world around you if you are always worried about money. If you can make smart decisions about money, you will learn to make meaningful choices in your life instead of being forced into situations because you are financially dependent on a job or a person or a place.

Making intelligent choices about money will teach you how to be satisfied with who you are and what you have instead of always wanting more. Imagine how happy we would all be if we could just be happy with what we have. Good luck, young money managers! Here's to a life of smart money choices.

If you've learned anything from this book, it's that having money smarts means that you think before you spend; you carefully plan your savings, and you are consistent in your money choices. It also means that you are disciplined and creative in the way you think about things that affect your wallet. You may find innovative ways to turn your computer skills or cooking talents into cold, hard cash. Or, you may be investing a chunk of your savings in bank CDs or mutual funds.

THE MIND-OVER-MONEY TEST

Here's a chance to test your newly found money knowledge. Don't sweat it if your score shows that you snoozed during a few sections of this book; just go back and review anytime you need to. It's never too late or too early to polish up your money skills. And there's sure to come a time when you'll be glad you did.

So, let's go:
1 If you get wise about money, you may be...
   a. setting money goals and developing a plan to help realize those goals.
   b. earning, saving, spending, investing, and donating your money.
   c. investing all your money in pork bellies.
   d. a and b.

❷ Making a mistake with money can happen to anyone. The important thing is to...

a. learn from the experience.

b. try harder to be the smartest consumer you can be.

c. save all your receipts for a time and keep track of your spending.

d. all of the above.

❸ Situations dealing with money and friends or family can get sticky. When money problems come up, it's best to...

a. sweep them under the rug.

b. avoid spending money for a fortnight (2 weeks).

c. talk about money issues right away to prevent bad feelings from surfacing.

d. a and c.

❹ Some things you need; some things you want. It's okay to want things, but limit them and make sure you...

a. can separate your needs from your wants.

b. reward yourself every once in a while.

c. can say no to yourself.

d. all of the above.

❺ You know how to be smart with your allowance:

a. It all gets banked, even if you have to mooch off others to get what you need.

b. Half of it goes toward snacks and drinks and the other half to movies and CDs.

c. A quarter of it goes for savings, a quarter of it goes for spending, a quarter of it goes for charities and birthday gifts for friends, and a quarter of it goes into your piggybank to be used for bus fare and snacks.

d. You save a third of it for the beginning of the week, a third of it for the middle of the week, and a third of it for the end of the week.

6 There are many ways to save money. Which of the following would not be a smart one?

   a. Buy your lunch in the school cafeteria every day.

   b. Swap CDs, videos, and books with friends.

   c. Check out secondhand stores.

   d. Clip coupons for items you and your family use.

7 Wise spending is...

   a. taking a wad of cash to the mall and making sure you spend it all in one place.

   b. going to your favorite store and making sure you buy at least one thing.

   c. comparison shopping at a few stores to find the best value and overall best buy.

   d. buying everything you can carry from your local discount store.

8 The very first step in setting up a budget is to make up...

   a. a list of everything you have ever wanted or needed.

   b. a list of all your income sources.

   c. a list of possible ways to cut corners when it comes to spending on others.

   d. all of the above.

Your Score

For each correct response, give yourself 2 points. A perfect score is 20 points.

1. d   **2.** d   **3.** c   **4.** d   **5.** c   **6.** a   **7.** c   **8.** b

What your answers mean:

1. Being wise about money means you've got a plan. It also means that you are dividing your earnings into these categories: savings, spending, investing, and donating.

2. When you make any mistake, the best thing to do is to learn from it. Combine that with smart consumerism and good record-keeping, and money smarts are sure to follow.

3. Talk it out. Most yucky feelings come back to haunt you when you sweep them under the rug. Being money smart means you're not afraid to discuss money matters and you're always looking for fair solutions.

4. Here's a recipe for $ success: Separate needs from wants, reward yourself now and again, and say no to yourself occasionally.

5. Think of your allowance as a pizza pie. Make sure to cut slices for savings, spending, charities, and presents. Also, make sure you cut a slice for transportation and snacks. The pizza will taste better that way!

6. Buying your lunch each day in the school cafeteria is definitely going to run you some bucks. Just imagine the savings if you could bring peanut butter and jelly sandwiches to school three times a week.

7. Shop around. That's the smartest advice any shopper can give or get.

8. The very first step in making a budget, before you do anything else, is finding out how much money you are bringing in. Then you will be able to tailor your wants and needs based on your income. The person bringing in a hundred dollars a week is going to have different wants and needs than the person bringing in ten dollars a week.

Your Score Card

0–4

Wake up! It's time to start thinking about money. Make a pact with yourself—think about money—ways to make it, save it, spend it, and share it—for 20 minutes a day. Take a trip to your local savings bank and watch all the action.

6–12

When it comes to your money skills, there's room for improvement, but don't sweat it, it's never too late to start. Learn five practical money tips a week and share them with your friends. Discuss the family budget with your parents.

14–16

Wow! When it comes to money sense, you are on top of things. Give yourself a hand. You really understand how money makes the world go 'round!

AFTERWORD

Euro-Ka! Did you hear the news? On the first day of the year, January 1, 2002, the euro was introduced, marking the biggest currency changeover the world has ever seen. Almost 300 million people in 12 countries turned in their bills and coins in exchange for brand-new euro banknotes (paper money) and coins. The new euro was circulated throughout Europe: Belgium, Germany, Greece, Spain, France, Ireland, Italy, Luxembourg, the Netherlands, Austria, Portugal, and Finland were the countries that traded in their old money for the euro. Just think of all the vending machines that had to be serviced to accept the new euro coins!

What were the 12 countries using before they switched for the euro? Here's a quiz to help you to remember the "old days" when they all used different money. Match up the country with the currency they used:

Country	Currency
1. Austria	**a.** lira
2. Belgium	**b.** escudo
3. Finland	**c.** franc
4. France	**d.** drachma
5. Germany	**e.** schilling
6. Greece	**f.** peseta
7. Ireland	**g.** franc
8. Italy	**h.** markka
9. Luxembourg	**i.** guilder
10. Netherlands	**j.** deutschmark
11. Portugal	**k.** franc
12. Spain	**l.** punt

Note: You have a good chance of doing well on this little quiz because, look again, three countries used currency called the "franc."

Answers: 1. e; 2. c; 3. h; 4. k; 5. j; 6. d; 7. l; 8. a; 9. g; 10. i; 11. b; 12. f.

LOOKING TOWARD THE FUTURE

So, why did they do it? Why did people want to change their currency? The euro came into being because the governments and business people in Europe wanted to make their economies and all their money transactions run smoother. The plan for the euro began back in 1957 when the Treaty of Rome called for the establishment of a common European market "to increase economic prosperity and contribute to an ever closer union among the peoples of Europe." And the euro is the answer? Think about it. What happened before the euro came along?

Before the euro

Imagine what it was like for an Italian doing business in France. First, the businessman had to exchange his lire (Italian currency before January 2002) for francs (French money before January 2002) before he could do business. Then he had to worry about the changing exchange rate (value of each currency up and down) that could end up costing him a lot of money to do business. (The exchange rate is based on the foreign exchange market and is constantly changing. Lists of exchange rates can be found in newspaper financial sections.)

Before the euro, tourists and vacationers from all parts of the world traveling through Europe had to change their money again and again—maybe twelve times—as they went from country to country! Can you imagine how confusing that was?

With the euro

The euro moves from one hand to another. Business is much smoother, and less time consuming. Tourists can use the same currency in 12 of the European countries, all thanks to the euro—and the people that looked ahead and worked to look into the future. Who's not part of the euro system? At this time, Denmark, Sweden, and the United Kingdom are members of the European Union, but are not using the euro.

THE EURO LOWDOWN

From design to distribution, years of planning and preparing went into creating the new money. The coins were designed by Luc Luycx of the Royal Belgian Mint,

Try this

Imagine you have been chosen to create a new coin for your country. What would it look like? What would it be made of? Whose picture or what image would be on it? Would you put any words on it? How much will the new coin be worth?

who won a European-wide competition to design them. Robert Kalina designed the banknotes. His design reflects the images of seven architectural periods from Europe's cultural history.

The coins have one side common to all 12 countries and a reverse side specific to each country. The eight denominations of coins—1, 2, 5, 10, 20, and 50 cent pieces—vary in size, color, and thickness. The banknotes look the same throughout the euro area. On the front of the banknotes, windows and gateways stand for the sharing and openness of the European countries, while the 12 stars of the European Union show the harmony among the nations. Each banknote also features a bridge, which represents communication and the spirit of cooperation between Europe and the rest of the world.

When creating a symbol for the euro, a design was needed that represented all of Europe. They wanted it to be attractive, but simple enough to be easily written by hand. The graphic symbol for the euro was inspired by the Greek letter *epsilon* and it refers to the first letter of the word Europe. The parallel lines represent the stability of the euro. The official abbreviation of the euro is EUR.

So, that's the story of the euro, the latest and biggest money news. What will happen to money in the future? Someday maybe the whole world will use only one kind of currency. Maybe we won't even need to touch money anymore, just carry a little coded card. Still, until money is a thing of the past, if you want to be sure to have the things you need to live and be happy, managing the money you make and spend will be an important part of your world. I hope that this book will be a help to you in making all your plans and dreams for the future come true.

INDEX

ABOUT THE AUTHOR

JAMIE KYLE MCGILLIAN, as a founding editor for Creative Classroom magazine, has written countless plays, short stories, and articles for young audiences, and many how-to articles for elementary teachers. She is the editor of *First-Time Teacher* magazine, a publication dedicated to giving new teachers a helping hand. She is the author of *Sidewalk Chalk: Outdoor Fun and Games* and *On the Job With a Firefighter.* An EdPress Award recipient who earns, saves, spends, invests, and donates in Westchester County, New York, McGillian teaches writing to fifth and sixth graders, and lives with her husband and two young daughters, Bailey and Devan.